SCRIPTURE
JOURNAL

ENGLISH STANDARD VERSION

1–3 JOHN

CROSSWAY

WHEATON, ILLINOIS — ESV.ORG

ESV® Scripture Journal: 1–3 John

The Holy Bible, English Standard Version® (ESV®)
Copyright © 2001 by Crossway,
a publishing ministry of Good News Publishers.
All rights reserved.

ESV® Text Edition: 2016

Printed in China
Published by Crossway
Wheaton, Illinois 60187, U.S.A.
crossway.org

Crossway is a not-for-profit publishing ministry that exists solely for the purpose of publishing the Good News of the Gospel and the Truth of God's Word, the Bible. A portion of the purchase price of every ESV Bible is donated to help support Bible distribution ministry around the world.

The ESV Bible is free online and on mobile devices everywhere worldwide, including a selection of free Bible resources, at esv.org.

RRDS	26	25	24	23	22	21	20	19	18	17
12	11	10	9	8	7	6	5	4	3	2	1

PREFACE

The Bible

The words of the Bible are the very words of God our Creator speaking to us. They are completely truthful;[1] they are pure;[2] they are powerful;[3] and they are wise and righteous.[4] We should read these words with reverence and awe,[5] and with joy and delight.[6] Through these words God gives us eternal life,[7] and daily nourishes our spiritual lives.[8]

The ESV Translation

The English Standard Version® (ESV®) stands in the classic stream of English Bible translations that goes back nearly five centuries. In this stream, accurate faithfulness to the original text is combined with simplicity, beauty, and dignity of expression. Our goal has been to carry forward this legacy for this generation and generations to come.

The ESV is an "essentially literal" translation that seeks as far as possible to reproduce the meaning and structure of the original text and the personal style of each Bible writer. We have sought to be "as literal as possible" while maintaining clear expression and literary excellence. Therefore the ESV is well suited for both personal reading and church ministry, for devotional reflection and serious study, and for Scripture memorization.

---

[1] Ps. 119:160; Prov. 30:5; Titus 1:2; Heb. 6:18 [2] Ps. 12:6 [3] Jer. 23:29; Heb. 4:12; 1 Pet. 1:23
[4] Ps. 19:7–11 [5] Deut. 28:58; Ps. 119:74; Isa. 66:2 [6] Ps. 19:7–11; 119:14, 97, 103; Jer. 15:16
[7] John 6:68; 1 Pet. 1:23 [8] Deut. 32:46; Matt. 4:4

The ESV Publishing Team

The ESV publishing team has included more than a hundred people. The fourteen-member Translation Oversight Committee benefited from the work of fifty biblical experts serving as Translation Review Scholars and from the comments of the more than fifty members of the Advisory Council. This international team from many denominations shares a common commitment to the truth of God's Word and to historic Christian orthodoxy.

To God's Honor and Praise

We know that no Bible translation is perfect; but we also know that God uses imperfect and inadequate things to his honor and praise. So to God the Father, Son, and Holy Spirit—and to his people—we offer what we have done, with our prayers that it may prove useful, with gratitude for much help given, and with ongoing wonder that our God should ever have entrusted to us so momentous a task.

To God alone be the glory!
The Translation Oversight Committee

1 JOHN

The Word of Life

1 That which was from the beginning, which we have heard, which we have seen with our eyes, which we looked upon and have touched with our hands, concerning the word of life— ² the life was made manifest, and we have seen it, and testify to it and proclaim to you the eternal life, which was with the Father and was made manifest to us— ³ that which we have seen and heard we proclaim also to you, so that you too may have fellowship with us; and indeed our fellowship is with the Father and with his Son Jesus Christ. ⁴ And we are writing these things so that our joy may be complete.

Walking in the Light

⁵ This is the message we have heard from him and proclaim to you, that God is light, and in him is no darkness at all. ⁶ If we say we have fellowship with him while we walk in darkness, we lie and do not practice the truth. ⁷ But if we walk in the light, as he is in the light, we have fellowship with one another, and the blood of Jesus his Son cleanses us from all sin. ⁸ If we say we have no sin, we deceive ourselves, and the truth is not in us. ⁹ If we confess our sins, he is faithful and just to forgive us our sins and to cleanse us from all unrighteousness. ¹⁰ If we say we have not sinned, we make him a liar, and his word is not in us.

Christ Our Advocate

2 My little children, I am writing these things to you so that you may not sin. But if anyone does sin, we have an advocate with the Father, Jesus Christ the righteous. ²He is the propitiation for our sins, and not for ours only but also for the sins of the whole world. ³And by this we know that we have come to know him, if we keep his commandments. ⁴Whoever says "I know him" but does not keep his commandments is a liar, and the truth is not in him, ⁵but whoever keeps his word, in him truly the love of God is perfected. By this we may know that we are in him: ⁶whoever says he abides in him ought to walk in the same way in which he walked.

The New Commandment

⁷Beloved, I am writing you no new commandment, but an old commandment that you had from the beginning. The old commandment is the word that you have heard. ⁸At the same time, it is a new commandment that I am writing to you, which is true in him and in you, because the darkness is passing away and the true light is already shining. ⁹Whoever says he is in the light and hates his brother is still in darkness. ¹⁰Whoever loves his brother abides in the light, and in him there is no cause for stumbling. ¹¹But whoever hates his brother is in the darkness and walks in the darkness, and does not know where he is going, because the darkness has blinded his eyes.

12   I am writing to you, little children,
            because your sins are forgiven for his name's sake.
13   I am writing to you, fathers,
            because you know him who is from the beginning.

I am writing to you, young men,
> because you have overcome the evil one.

I write to you, children,
> because you know the Father.

14 I write to you, fathers,
> because you know him who is from the beginning.

I write to you, young men,
> because you are strong,
> and the word of God abides in you,
> and you have overcome the evil one.

Do Not Love the World

¹⁵ Do not love the world or the things in the world. If anyone loves the world, the love of the Father is not in him. ¹⁶ For all that is in the world—the desires of the flesh and the desires of the eyes and pride of life—is not from the Father but is from the world. ¹⁷ And the world is passing away along with its desires, but whoever does the will of God abides forever.

Warning Concerning Antichrists

¹⁸ Children, it is the last hour, and as you have heard that antichrist is coming, so now many antichrists have come. Therefore we know that it is the last hour. ¹⁹ They went out from us, but they were not of us; for if they had been of us, they would have continued with us. But they went out, that it might become plain that they all are not of us. ²⁰ But you have been anointed by the Holy One, and you all have knowledge. ²¹ I write to you, not because you do not know the truth, but because you know it, and because no lie is of the truth. ²² Who is the liar but he who denies that Jesus is the Christ? This is the

antichrist, he who denies the Father and the Son. ²³ No one who
denies the Son has the Father. Whoever confesses the Son has
the Father also. ²⁴ Let what you heard from the beginning abide
in you. If what you heard from the beginning abides in you,
then you too will abide in the Son and in the Father. ²⁵ And this
is the promise that he made to us—eternal life.

²⁶ I write these things to you about those who are trying to
deceive you. ²⁷ But the anointing that you received from him
abides in you, and you have no need that anyone should teach
you. But as his anointing teaches you about everything, and is
true, and is no lie—just as it has taught you, abide in him.

Children of God

²⁸ And now, little children, abide in him, so that when he
appears we may have confidence and not shrink from him in
shame at his coming. ²⁹ If you know that he is righteous, you
may be sure that everyone who practices righteousness has
been born of him.

3 See what kind of love the Father has given to us, that we
should be called children of God; and so we are. The reason
why the world does not know us is that it did not know him.
² Beloved, we are God's children now, and what we will be has
not yet appeared; but we know that when he appears we shall
be like him, because we shall see him as he is. ³ And everyone
who thus hopes in him purifies himself as he is pure.

⁴ Everyone who makes a practice of sinning also practices
lawlessness; sin is lawlessness. ⁵ You know that he appeared in
order to take away sins, and in him there is no sin. ⁶ No one who
abides in him keeps on sinning; no one who keeps on sinning
has either seen him or known him. ⁷ Little children, let no one

deceive you. Whoever practices righteousness is righteous, as he is righteous. [8] Whoever makes a practice of sinning is of the devil, for the devil has been sinning from the beginning. The reason the Son of God appeared was to destroy the works of the devil. [9] No one born of God makes a practice of sinning, for God's seed abides in him; and he cannot keep on sinning, because he has been born of God. [10] By this it is evident who are the children of God, and who are the children of the devil: whoever does not practice righteousness is not of God, nor is the one who does not love his brother.

Love One Another

[11] For this is the message that you have heard from the beginning, that we should love one another. [12] We should not be like Cain, who was of the evil one and murdered his brother. And why did he murder him? Because his own deeds were evil and his brother's righteous. [13] Do not be surprised, brothers, that the world hates you. [14] We know that we have passed out of death into life, because we love the brothers. Whoever does not love abides in death. [15] Everyone who hates his brother is a murderer, and you know that no murderer has eternal life abiding in him.

[16] By this we know love, that he laid down his life for us, and we ought to lay down our lives for the brothers. [17] But if anyone has the world's goods and sees his brother in need, yet closes his heart against him, how does God's love abide in him? [18] Little children, let us not love in word or talk but in deed and in truth.

[19] By this we shall know that we are of the truth and reassure our heart before him; [20] for whenever our heart condemns

us, God is greater than our heart, and he knows everything. [21] Beloved, if our heart does not condemn us, we have confidence before God; [22] and whatever we ask we receive from him, because we keep his commandments and do what pleases him. [23] And this is his commandment, that we believe in the name of his Son Jesus Christ and love one another, just as he has commanded us. [24] Whoever keeps his commandments abides in God, and God in him. And by this we know that he abides in us, by the Spirit whom he has given us.

Test the Spirits

4 Beloved, do not believe every spirit, but test the spirits to see whether they are from God, for many false prophets have gone out into the world. [2] By this you know the Spirit of God: every spirit that confesses that Jesus Christ has come in the flesh is from God, [3] and every spirit that does not confess Jesus is not from God. This is the spirit of the antichrist, which you heard was coming and now is in the world already. [4] Little children, you are from God and have overcome them, for he who is in you is greater than he who is in the world. [5] They are from the world; therefore they speak from the world, and the world listens to them. [6] We are from God. Whoever knows God listens to us; whoever is not from God does not listen to us. By this we know the Spirit of truth and the spirit of error.

God Is Love

[7] Beloved, let us love one another, for love is from God, and whoever loves has been born of God and knows God. [8] Anyone who does not love does not know God, because God is love. [9] In this the love of God was made manifest among us, that God

sent his only Son into the world, so that we might live through him. [10] In this is love, not that we have loved God but that he loved us and sent his Son to be the propitiation for our sins. [11] Beloved, if God so loved us, we also ought to love one another. [12] No one has ever seen God; if we love one another, God abides in us and his love is perfected in us.

[13] By this we know that we abide in him and he in us, because he has given us of his Spirit. [14] And we have seen and testify that the Father has sent his Son to be the Savior of the world. [15] Whoever confesses that Jesus is the Son of God, God abides in him, and he in God. [16] So we have come to know and to believe the love that God has for us. God is love, and whoever abides in love abides in God, and God abides in him. [17] By this is love perfected with us, so that we may have confidence for the day of judgment, because as he is so also are we in this world. [18] There is no fear in love, but perfect love casts out fear. For fear has to do with punishment, and whoever fears has not been perfected in love. [19] We love because he first loved us. [20] If anyone says, "I love God," and hates his brother, he is a liar; for he who does not love his brother whom he has seen cannot love God whom he has not seen. [21] And this commandment we have from him: whoever loves God must also love his brother.

Overcoming the World

5 Everyone who believes that Jesus is the Christ has been born of God, and everyone who loves the Father loves whoever has been born of him. [2] By this we know that we love the children of God, when we love God and obey his commandments. [3] For this is the love of God, that we keep his commandments. And his commandments are not burdensome. [4] For everyone

who has been born of God overcomes the world. And this is the victory that has overcome the world—our faith. ⁵Who is it that overcomes the world except the one who believes that Jesus is the Son of God?

Testimony Concerning the Son of God

⁶This is he who came by water and blood—Jesus Christ; not by the water only but by the water and the blood. And the Spirit is the one who testifies, because the Spirit is the truth. ⁷For there are three that testify: ⁸the Spirit and the water and the blood; and these three agree. ⁹If we receive the testimony of men, the testimony of God is greater, for this is the testimony of God that he has borne concerning his Son. ¹⁰Whoever believes in the Son of God has the testimony in himself. Whoever does not believe God has made him a liar, because he has not believed in the testimony that God has borne concerning his Son. ¹¹And this is the testimony, that God gave us eternal life, and this life is in his Son. ¹²Whoever has the Son has life; whoever does not have the Son of God does not have life.

That You May Know

¹³I write these things to you who believe in the name of the Son of God, that you may know that you have eternal life. ¹⁴And this is the confidence that we have toward him, that if we ask anything according to his will he hears us. ¹⁵And if we know that he hears us in whatever we ask, we know that we have the requests that we have asked of him.

¹⁶If anyone sees his brother committing a sin not leading to death, he shall ask, and God will give him life—to those who commit sins that do not lead to death. There is sin that leads to

death; I do not say that one should pray for that. [17] All wrong-doing is sin, but there is sin that does not lead to death.

[18] We know that everyone who has been born of God does not keep on sinning, but he who was born of God protects him, and the evil one does not touch him.

[19] We know that we are from God, and the whole world lies in the power of the evil one.

[20] And we know that the Son of God has come and has given us understanding, so that we may know him who is true; and we are in him who is true, in his Son Jesus Christ. He is the true God and eternal life. [21] Little children, keep yourselves from idols.

2 JOHN

Greeting

¹ The elder to the elect lady and her children, whom I love in truth, and not only I, but also all who know the truth, ² because of the truth that abides in us and will be with us forever:

³ Grace, mercy, and peace will be with us, from God the Father and from Jesus Christ the Father's Son, in truth and love.

Walking in Truth and Love

⁴ I rejoiced greatly to find some of your children walking in the truth, just as we were commanded by the Father. ⁵ And now I ask you, dear lady—not as though I were writing you a new commandment, but the one we have had from the beginning—that we love one another. ⁶ And this is love, that we walk according to his commandments; this is the commandment, just as you have heard from the beginning, so that you should walk in it. ⁷ For many deceivers have gone out into the world, those who do not confess the coming of Jesus Christ in the flesh. Such a one is the deceiver and the antichrist. ⁸ Watch yourselves, so that you may not lose what we have worked for, but may win a full reward. ⁹ Everyone who goes on ahead and does not abide in the teaching of Christ, does not have God. Whoever abides in the teaching has both the Father and the Son. ¹⁰ If anyone comes to you and does not bring this teaching,

do not receive him into your house or give him any greeting, [11] for whoever greets him takes part in his wicked works.

Final Greetings

[12] Though I have much to write to you, I would rather not use paper and ink. Instead I hope to come to you and talk face to face, so that our joy may be complete.

[13] The children of your elect sister greet you.

3 JOHN

Greeting

¹ The elder to the beloved Gaius, whom I love in truth.

² Beloved, I pray that all may go well with you and that you may be in good health, as it goes well with your soul. ³ For I rejoiced greatly when the brothers came and testified to your truth, as indeed you are walking in the truth. ⁴ I have no greater joy than to hear that my children are walking in the truth.

Support and Opposition

⁵ Beloved, it is a faithful thing you do in all your efforts for these brothers, strangers as they are, ⁶ who testified to your love before the church. You will do well to send them on their journey in a manner worthy of God. ⁷ For they have gone out for the sake of the name, accepting nothing from the Gentiles. ⁸ Therefore we ought to support people like these, that we may be fellow workers for the truth.

⁹ I have written something to the church, but Diotrephes, who likes to put himself first, does not acknowledge our authority. ¹⁰ So if I come, I will bring up what he is doing, talking wicked nonsense against us. And not content with that, he refuses to welcome the brothers, and also stops those who want to and puts them out of the church.

[11] Beloved, do not imitate evil but imitate good. Whoever does good is from God; whoever does evil has not seen God. [12] Demetrius has received a good testimony from everyone, and from the truth itself. We also add our testimony, and you know that our testimony is true.

Final Greetings

[13] I had much to write to you, but I would rather not write with pen and ink. [14] I hope to see you soon, and we will talk face to face.

[15] Peace be to you. The friends greet you. Greet the friends, each by name.